IMAGES
of America

THE PALACE
HOTEL

IMAGES
of America

THE PALACE HOTEL

Richard Harned

ARCADIA
PUBLISHING

Published by Arcadia Publishing
Charleston, South Carolina

Printed in the United States of America

Library of Congress Catalog Card Number: 2008930696

For all general information contact Arcadia Publishing at:
Telephone 843-853-2070
Fax 843-853-0044
E-mail sales@arcadiapublishing.com
For customer service and orders:
Toll-Free 1-888-313-2665

Visit us on the Internet at www.arcadiapublishing.com

This book is dedicated to William Chapman Ralston, the man who built San Francisco.

CONTENTS

ACKNOWLEDGMENTS

I wish to express my gratitude to the following people for their assistance in helping me complete this book. My thanks to the management of the Palace Hotel, especially the keeper of their historic photograph collection, chief engineer Jerry Turner, for sharing this priceless resource with me. Unless otherwise noted, all images in this book are from the archives of the Palace Hotel. Thanks also to the entire staff of the San Francisco Public Library's San Francisco History Center (SFPL) and their wonderful San Francisco Historic Photograph Collection. Special thanks to my editor, John Poultney, who not only gave me the idea for the book but also kept faith in the project to its conclusion. I would also like to thank Rob Spoor, the guru of City Guides' Palace Hotel tour guides, who taught me most of what I know about the history of the hotel. Thanks also to fellow city guides Pam Ferrero, who shared her Palace Hotel postcard collection with me, and Sylvia Stress, who also answered my call for assistance in finding additional images. And last, but certainly not least, I want to thank my wife, Pauline, for her moral support, helpful hints, and endless love.

INTRODUCTION

When San Francisco's Palace Hotel first opened its doors in 1875, it was the largest hotel in the world. This achievement is even more remarkable when you consider that the population of San Francisco in 1848 was approximately 500 people. In order to fully understand how this extraordinary event took place, it is necessary to understand the history of the area itself.

To begin with, the area now known as California remained in a state of isolation for several centuries after the rest of the world was being "discovered" by European explorers. The area was first inhabited by native peoples, who probably migrated from Asia across the Bering land bridge and settled into a land where flora and fauna were plentiful and the mild climate allowed them to live year-round with only moderate seasonal migrations. The various native groups had limited contact with each other, which was perpetuated by the development of separate languages as different as Spanish is to English.

While various European naval explorers, including Juan Rodríguez Cabrillo, Sebastian Vizcaíno, and Sir Francis Drake, all sailed along the California coastline and even made small incursions along the shoreline, none of them spotted the Golden Gate's entrance into San Francisco Bay. Although Spain had a claim on this land that they called Alta California, they never attempted to colonize the area until the Russian fur companies' continued southward expansion from Alaska brought them deep into Alta California. In 1769, the Spanish began their effort to colonize California by building a mission in San Diego, the first of 21 missions they would eventually build in Alta California. From there, they sent an exploration party to find a site for a mission in the vicinity of Monterey Bay, which Vizcaíno had described in his 1602 voyage. This exploration party passed Monterey Bay without recognizing it and continued their march northward until they eventually spotted San Francisco Bay. Based on this finding, the Spanish decided to also colonize the San Francisco Bay area, and a group of colonists arrived in San Francisco on June 27, 1776, seven days before the Declaration of Independence was signed on the other side of the North American continent.

Because San Francisco Bay was the northernmost part of the Spanish empire, the isolation factor continued into the 19th century. The Spanish had their hands full with wars in Europe and insurrections in Latin America and made little further progress in settling Alta California. Then, when the Louisiana Purchase was made in 1803, the western movement of the United States began in earnest. After the Lewis and Clark Expedition publicized the westward expansion of the United States, the Manifest Destiny movement began to swell, and it became an assumption by many that the United States would eventually extend from "sea to shining sea."

Meanwhile, political change was also being realized in Alta California. After Mexico achieved its independence from Spain in 1821, Alta California became a possession of Mexico. While Spain had prohibited trade with other nations for fear of losing Alta California, the Mexican government encouraged such commerce, and the isolation factor began to weaken. After Mexico disbanded the Spanish mission program in 1833, the mission lands were secularized, vast land grants were awarded, and the era of the rancho began. Because the rancho lands were ideal for the raising of cattle, a lucrative trade in beef, hides, and tallow began to flourish, and the United States became a major trading partner with Mexico. In 1834, the United States offered to buy the San Francisco Bay area as home base for American whalers in the Pacific, but Mexico declined the offer.

However, the government of Mexico was experiencing problems in other parts of their realm that would eventually affect Alta California. After Mexico's Pres. Antonio López de Santa Anna suspended the constitution and disbanded the congress, many of the Mexican states revolted against the federal government. In March 1836, Texas declared its independence from Mexico, and the Republic of Texas was born. In 1845, both the U.S. Congress and the Congress of Texas voted for the annexation of Texas by the United States. Mexico had never relinquished its claim to Texas, and the U.S. annexation of Texas precipitated the Mexican War in May 1846.

Meanwhile, in Alta California, a group of American settlers in the Sonoma area captured the Mexican commandant, Gen. Mariano Vallejo, and declared the establishment of the California Republic. Shortly thereafter, the U.S. Navy's fleet under the command of Commodore John Sloat learned of the Sonoma revolt and the outbreak of hostilities in Texas and sent the marines ashore to raise the American flag at Monterey on July 7, 1846, and at San Francisco five days later. With that, the Mexican province of Alta California remained under the control of the U.S. military until February 2, 1848, when the Treaty of Guadalupe Hidalgo ended the war and Mexico ceded to the United States all of its land north of the Rio Grande.

At virtually the same time, on January 24, 1848, John Marshall discovered gold in the American River, north of Sacramento. The official announcement of the gold discovery by President Polk in late 1848 would trigger one of the largest peacetime mass migrations of people ever recorded in history. The influx of forty-niners would soon overwhelm the entire social order of Northern California, and lands owned by the rancheros and Native American tribes would be taken over by armed gold seekers. Thus, in a very brief period of time, the area that became the state of California had become the imperial pawn for a dizzying succession of landlords—from the governments of Spain, Mexico, and the United States to an avalanche of people coming to seek their fortunes.

One

THE GILDED ERA

At the time of the discovery of gold in California in 1848, San Francisco was little more than a frontier town, with a population of approximately 500 people. The above photograph of Montgomery Street shows the Russ House in the location where the Russ Building stands today. At that time, the quickest way to get to California from anywhere in the world was by ship, and San Francisco Bay was the harbor closest to the goldfields. By the end of 1849, San Francisco had become an instant city, with a population of nearly 20,000. While most of the new arrivals stayed in San Francisco only briefly before heading to the goldfields to seek their fortunes, many others acquired considerable wealth by outfitting the gold seekers. William Ralston was one of those profiteers. (SFPL.)

William Chapman Ralston was born in Wellsville, Ohio, in 1826. At the age of 23, Ralston decided to seek his fortune in California and joined the Gold Rush in 1849. Instead of sailing around the Horn, he opted for the shorter but more expensive route across the Isthmus of Panama and spent the rest of the Gold Rush in the profitable business of transporting other gold seekers to El Dorado. When he finally arrived in San Francisco in 1854, the Gold Rush was over, but Ralston had amassed enough money to start a banking enterprise that would become the Bank of California in 1864. Although he was always the driving force behind the bank, Ralston modestly assumed the title of cashier for the bank. The Bank of California opened just in time to finance the mine owners in Virginia City, Nevada, where silver was discovered in the famous Comstock Lode. (SFPL.)

After the gold deposits along the American River had been exhausted, the miners continued their search across the Sierras and beyond for the precious metal. One of those outlying areas was Virginia City, Nevada, named after an early prospector from the state of Virginia. Another early prospector was Henry Comstock, who acquired part ownership of a mining claim and had the silver deposit named after him. While the amount of gold discovered in that location was enough to encourage early miners, the mining process was complicated by the existence of a bluish ore that clogged the rockers used by the miners. Eventually, a sample of this foreign matter was taken to an assay office, where it was determined to be a high grade of silver. With that, the rush to the Comstock began.

Although San Francisco was still little more than a frontier town, Ralston was convinced it was destined to become a world-class city; he went on to become known as "the man who built San Francisco." He would personally sit down with anyone who came into the bank with a proposal for the betterment of San Francisco and would reward the sound proposals with a loan, utilizing the proceeds from the Comstock to secure these investments. Usually, the loan would be provided directly by the bank; in other instances, Ralston would finance the loan from his own account. Ralston had a tendency to blur the distinction between his money and that of the bank, something that would come back to haunt him later on. In addition to funding the projects of others, he had a number of pet projects of his own, foremost of which would be the Palace Hotel.

The entire history of the Comstock Lode was marked by periods of boom or bust. The initial boom period ended when all of the silver near the surface had been mined. In order to pursue the vein of silver deeper into the mountain, the mine owners would have to sink mine shafts, dig tunnels, and install machinery to get the ore and the miners out of the mines. All of this would require a great deal of capital up front, and the Bank of California opened just in time to provide that capital. Soon, because the bank was doing so much business with the mine owners in Virginia City, Ralston decided to open a branch bank there, and he chose Sen. William Sharon to manage that branch. Sharon, a very shrewd businessman, would offer loans at interest rates half of that charged by other banks and accept shares of the mines as collateral. When subsequent bust periods kept the mine owners from repaying their loans, Sharon would foreclose and take over ownership of the mines. (SFPL.)

John W. Mackay

While the Bank of California continued to tighten its monopoly over the wealth of the Comstock, four Irish immigrants in San Francisco would soon realize the "luck of the Irish." John Mackay (pictured here) and James Fair were both experienced operators in the Comstock Lode, and both agreed it would be a good gamble to try to gain control of the Hale and Norcross Mine, one the mines controlled by the Bank of California. To do this, they formed a partnership with James Flood and William O'Brien, who had recently established themselves as traders in Comstock stocks at the San Francisco Mining Exchange. They quietly began to acquire shares of the Hale and Norcross Mine, and before Sharon realized what was happening, the future "Silver Kings" had wrested control of the mine that would soon produce the "Big Bonanza," the richest strike of precious metals in mining history. (SFPL.)

Homes of Mark Hopkins and Leland Stanford–Hill of the Nabobs ("Nob") SF.

In 1876, the *San Francisco Examiner* listed more than 200 San Franciscans worth over $1 million. In addition to the wealthy Silver Kings, the completion of the transcontinental railroad also fostered instant wealth to those who participated in the management side of its construction, especially the owners of the Central Pacific Railroad: Leland Stanford, Collis Huntington, Mark Hopkins, and Charles Crocker, known collectively as the Big Four. Nearly all had started from modest beginnings, and the sudden accumulation of great wealth was more than some could handle modestly. The invention of the cable car had opened Nob Hill to development, and the suddenly rich began a building boom of monumental proportions. The Leland Stanfords were the first of the newly rich to occupy Nob Hill, and their $2-million mansion was completed in 1874. Not to be outdone, Mrs. Mark Hopkins (Mary) countered with a bizarre concoction of Victorian decor that would become the most extravagant edifice on the hill. Their mansions were located at the sites of the two hotels bearing their names today. (SFPL.)

Another of the Big Four, Charles Crocker, constructed his mansion (left) at the site of today's Grace Cathedral. Next door was the house of David Colton (right), a lawyer for the Big Four. This was probably the most restrained of the Nob Hill mansions. When Colton died, the Big Four sued his widow for the remainder of his fortune, claiming it was money that Colton had embezzled from the railroad. At the trial, Mrs. Colton vindicated her husband's name by introducing as evidence the "Colton Letters," exposing the machinations by which the Big Four had acquired their wealth. Not shown in the photograph was a modest structure next to the Colton mansion that was the home of one of the original settlers of Nob Hill, Nicholas Yung. When Yung refused to sell his property to Charles Crocker, the latter built a 40-foot-high "spite fence" around Yung's dwelling. (SFPL.)

William Ralston also joined in the competition for the most luxurious home of the Gilded Era. While his San Francisco residence was quite elegant, Ralston's showplace was located about 25 miles south of San Francisco, in what is now the city of Belmont. Ralston purchased the estate of the Italian count Leonetto Cipriani and immediately began to make additions and improvements to the property. He added a large dining room and ballroom to the main structure, which resembled the Hall of Mirrors at Versailles. The manor house contained over 100 rooms, including 50 bedrooms. Adjoining the manor were tennis courts, a bowling alley, and livery stables. An ardent horseman, Ralston used to frequently load his invited guests onto the train in San Francisco and race his guests to his estate, changing horses along the way. Ralston Hall is the sole visual reminder of Ralston's many contributions and is now part of the campus of Notre Dame de Namur University.

There was one San Franciscan who became a millionaire from the Comstock who did not invest his good fortune in self indulgence. That man was Adolph Sutro, who came to San Francisco from Germany in 1850. He relocated to the Comstock and opened a stamping mill. Because of the thermal activity below Virginia City, the working conditions for the miners were dismal. Sutro designed and built a tunnel beneath the principal mine shafts that provided drainage, ventilation, and an escape route for the miners. He then sold his shares of the tunnel and moved back to San Francisco, where he purchased approximately 11 percent of all of the land in San Francisco, primarily in the area west of Twin Peaks. He used portions of his land to construct the Sutro Baths as a source of recreation for the people of San Francisco. He also donated the land for the University of California medical school, located on Mount Sutro. As gratitude for his many acts of noblesse oblige, he was elected mayor of San Francisco in 1894. (SFPL.)

The building boom in San Francisco was not restricted to homes and businesses but extended to the construction of hotels as well. Under the influence of the wealth of the Comstock, several luxury hotels were also constructed in San Francisco during the Gilded Era. One of the early luxury hotels was the Baldwin Hotel, located on Market Street. The hotel was named for and built by Elias "Lucky" Baldwin, who acquired his fortune from investments in trading in Comstock stocks. When Baldwin left San Francisco on a worldwide journey, he left instructions with his attorney to sell his stocks if the price fell below a certain level. When that level was reached, the attorney realized the stocks were locked in Baldwin's safe, for which he lacked the combination. By the time Baldwin returned, the value of the stocks had increased dramatically, and Baldwin was always known thereafter as "Lucky." (SFPL.)

Another early luxury hotel, the Grand Hotel, was built by William Ralston. The hotel was located on the south side of Market Street, on the corner of what would become New Montgomery Street. By this time, San Francisco's business district extended down Montgomery Street as far as Market, and the visionary Ralston began purchasing property south of Market, believing that would be the direction of future expansion. While the Grand Hotel was luxurious by San Francisco standards of the time, it lacked the stature of a world-class hotel. When Ralston was guiding a European dignitary through the hotel, the visitor sniffed, "This hotel does not seem so grand." He was wounded by the insult, and Ralston's building aspirations were further challenged. Believing every world-class city had to have a world-class hotel, Ralston vowed the Palace Hotel would fulfill that role for San Francisco. (SFPL.)

The discovery of the Big Bonanza prompted Ralston, Sharon, and others to speculate wildly on shares of adjacent mines in hopes that the vein of silver would extend in one of those directions. When these efforts appeared fruitless, Sharon quietly unloaded all of his shares onto the market, leaving Ralston with a portfolio of worthless stock. Sharon's action was interpreted as a desperate act to save the bank, causing a panic and a run on the Bank of California. On August 26, 1875, the Bank of California had to close its doors early because it had literally run out of money. The board of directors ordered an audit and discovered Ralston was approximately $9 million in debt, including $5 million he had borrowed from the bank without bothering to tell anyone. The board of directors forced Ralston to resign from the bank and sell everything he owned to Bill Sharon for $5 million so he could repay the bank. With that, Ralston was ruined. (SFPL.)

On that same afternoon, Ralston walked to North Beach to take his customary swim in the bay. After changing into his bathing suit, he started swimming in the direction of Alcatraz and died. The immediate assumption by everyone was that, in his shame, Ralston had swum as far as he was physically able and intentionally drowned. The coroner performed an autopsy and did not find enough water in the lungs to constitute drowning. Ralston's death was ruled as accidental, probably caused by a stroke. The funeral held for Billy Ralston was attended by approximately 50,000 people, the largest funeral in the history of San Francisco. The funeral procession was said to have extended for nearly 6 miles. The photograph above is the memorial erected to Ralston on the Marina Green, overlooking San Francisco Bay. (SFPL.)

Two

The First Palace Hotel

ORPHAN ASYLUM AND ST. PATRICK'S CHURCH IN 1865 *1856*
The Palace Hotel, Market Street, is built on the site they occupied

The first Palace Hotel was located on the same spot where the present hotel stands today, at the corner of Market and New Montgomery Streets. This area was originally known as Happy Valley, named after a group of squatters who first settled there, apparently best known for their joyous lifestyle. After the squatters were evicted, the land was purchased by the Catholic Church, which built St. Patrick's Church and an orphanage there, as shown in the photograph above. Ralston first began the purchase of the land as a site for the Grand Hotel. Eventually, he acquired the entire block at a total cost of $400,000. (SFPL.)

Architect John P. Gaynor was hired to design the first Palace Hotel. After studying the construction of the leading American hotels on the East Coast and in Europe, Gaynor returned to San Francisco, and excavation of the site began in 1873. The general plan for the building was that of a rectangle, covering an area of 2.5 acres. The long (350 foot) sides of the rectangle would face New Montgomery and Annie Streets, with the shorter (275 foot) sides on Market and Jessie Streets. The photograph above shows the hotel and a few of the neighboring buildings. The photograph below depicts the Palace and Grand Hotels facing each other across New Montgomery Street. (Both, SFPL.)

When the first hotel opened in 1875, it was the largest hotel in the world. It was seven stories high and covered an entire block. Its outer walls, of brick, averaged 2 feet in thickness. The hotel, when finished, contained 31 million bricks and 10 million feet of lumber. During construction, there were often 300 bricklayers at work, each of whom laid about 1,500 bricks per day. In order to ensure an adequate supply of bricks and lumber, Ralston built his own brickyard in Oakland and also purchased an entire oak forest in the Sierra foothills to provide wood for floors and paneling in the various rooms and suites. Pictured in the photograph is the Market Street side of the first Palace Hotel and Lotta's Fountain, which was erected in 1875 and still stands today.

The main entrance to the hotel was a carriage entrance located on New Montgomery Street. Arriving guests would be driven inside the building and deposited in the midst of a forest of potted plants onto a marble-paved floor, measuring 84 by 144 feet and shaped like a keyhole. The courtyard was surrounded by seven floors of balustrades and covered by a soaring roof of opaque glass. The inside corridors on each floor opened onto the courtyard, allowing the guests to promenade along the corridors, peering into the courtyard to see who was coming or going. This was "the place" to be seen in San Francisco. The photograph above shows a number of guests and their carriages in the courtyard, and pictured below is the top floor of the hotel. (Below, SFPL.)

After awhile, the hotel management began to receive complaints from the guests concerning the odor and the noise made by the horses. The problem became worse with the advent of automobiles, which were even smellier and noisier than the horses. Moreover, the turning radius of the automobiles of that time would not allow them to make a U-turn within the courtyard, so they would have to depart by backing into New Montgomery Street. Shortly after 1900, the carriage entrance was closed, and the space it had occupied was covered with marble tiles. In the photograph above, the courtyard was converted into a lounge known as the Grand Court, which would become the prototype for the Garden Court in the hotel today.

The conversion from carriage entrance to Grand Court was also captured in early postcards. In the image at left, a single date palm graces the original carriage entrance. Below, the carriage entrance has been eliminated, and the space has been transformed into the Grand Court.

Date Palm in Court of Palace Hotel - San Francisco

The Palace Hotel, San Francisco, Cal.

The first hotel contained 755 guest rooms, with accommodations for 1,200 guests. Most of the guest rooms were 20 feet square, with 15-foot ceilings. Each of the guest rooms had its own water closet. Each room also had an electric call button, which summoned the hotel staff via 125 miles of wire. In 1875, telephones and electric lights were still too primitive for practical operation and would be added later. As shown in the photograph above, each of the outside rooms had bay windows to provide maximum daylight on foggy days. Each guest room had its own fireplace and was also equipped with a primitive air-conditioning system to carry off any lingering smoke. Each floor had a "tubular conductor" to carry outgoing and incoming mail and messages to various locations within the hotel.

Drawing Room Suite

Most of the furnishings were locally made, and a furniture factory was built by Ralston to augment the facilities in existence on the West Coast. Ralston also purchased door lock and key companies to furnish the vast quantities of those commodities needed for the hotel. The amount of marble used in the hotel was so great that contracts had to be made with 15 different firms to create 800 mantels, 900 washstands, and 40,000 square feet of flooring. Finishing woods of ebony, teak, and rosewood were imported from around the world; much of it was hand carved and all was highly polished. To supply and install the acres of carpets, the firm of W. and J. Sloane, of New York, established a local store to service the hotel and remained in business in San Francisco after the hotel was completed.

The hotel's common areas were also enormous. The lobby and the office area pictured above measured 65 by 55 feet and had a 25-foot ceiling. The main dining room shown below was 150 feet long. On the Market Street side of the hotel, space had been provided for 18 retail stores. Each had two entrances and two sets of show windows, one facing the street and the other on long galleries within the building. Guests could thus enjoy the luxury of doing their shopping without having to leave the hotel. (Above, SFPL.)

The Palace was the first hotel on the West Coast to have hydraulic elevators, four for passengers and one for freight. The elevators were so large they were called "rising rooms." Each could hold 30–40 passengers sitting and enjoying tea service on the way to their rooms. One local newspaper lampooned that the elevators also contained pianos and bowling alleys. The main bar pictured above and the adjoining billiard room shown below were not only huge but ornate. Notice the marble facing on the front of the bar, the inlaid bar surface, the galleria ceiling, and the winged figures on each corner of the bar. Below the bar rail are some of the 9,000 cuspidors made for the hotel.

The hotel's first chef, pictured above, was Jules Harder, who became the West Coast's authority on all matters pertaining to food and its service. Before coming to the Palace, Harder had 26 years' experience in hotels, clubs, and restaurants, including 10 years at Delmonico in New York. The Palace was mainly responsible for spreading knowledge of distinctly California foods. Included on the menu were quail, venison, and even grizzly steaks. The California oyster omelet became one of the featured items on the menu. An equally famous concoction was "pudding a'la Sultan," the creation of another early Palace chef, Ernest Arbogast. One of the early and continuing traditions of the Palace Hotel was a Christmas dinner, which usually lasted for hours.

When the hotel opened, its kitchen and serving staffs were the largest of any hotel in the country. One hundred and fifty waiters served guests in the hotel's three dining rooms. Pictured here is the Men's Grill.

Here is the Ladies' Grill. The requirement for 9,000 table settings in the main dining area was made on special order by C. F. Haviland, France. In addition, the hotel had a "gold service" sufficient to serve 100 guests for very special occasions. One such occasion was the Banquet of the Golden Plate, held for Pres. Theodore Roosevelt. In addition to the 100 place settings, the gold service included specialty items like toothpick holders and napkin rings.

This photograph of the first Palace Hotel was taken in 1906, shortly before the great earthquake and fire that year. At lower left is a covered bridge that had been added to the hotel, connecting the Palace Hotel with the Grand Hotel across New Montgomery Street. The stated purpose of the covered bridge was to allow hotel guests to go from one hotel to the other without being impacted by inclement weather. It also allowed the gentlemen to have a room in the Palace Hotel and their female escorts in the Grand Hotel and to allow passage without being seen in the lobby. The bridge was known colloquially as the "bridge of sighs."

This early sketch captures the excitement of the hotel's opening, plus the bustle and opulence

of the growing city.

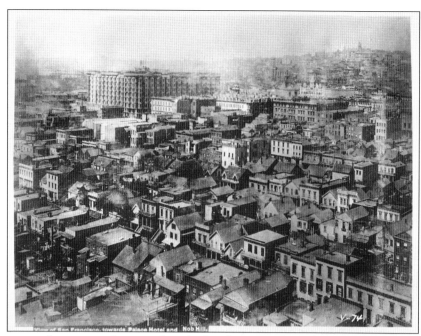

Within a year of opening, it became clear the hotel was simply too large. Despite its continuing growth, San Francisco had a surplus of hotels and certainly did not require a behemoth with 800 rooms. It would be many years before all of the hotel's guest rooms would be sold out. At the same time, the supply of luxury homes in the city could not keep pace with the swelling numbers of the newly rich. The solution to both of these problems was found by converting the surplus rooms at the hotel into luxury apartments. After Bill Sharon's wife, Maria, died, Sharon moved from the estate in Belmont and established an apartment at the hotel. Leland Stanford also occupied a suite while his mansion on Nob Hill was being constructed. The permanent guests, some of whom are pictured below, were quartered on the top two floors, where they constituted a separate social group. Bill Sharon died in the hotel on November 13, 1885, and his funeral was held in one of the hotel's parlors three days later. (Both, SFPL.)

Three

THE 1906 EARTHQUAKE AND FIRE

Most earthquakes occur along the boundaries of the huge plates that cover the surface of the earth. The San Andreas Fault forms the boundary between the Pacific plate, which is moving north, and the North American plate, which is moving west. California is slowly being torn apart along the San Andreas Fault. Between 1850 and 1905, it is estimated that San Francisco experienced approximately 465 earthquakes, most of them minor. The city's only major quake during that time occurred in 1868. Because of that, the threat of a major earthquake was fully taken into account by architect John Gaynor in his design of the Palace Hotel. The first hotel stood on massive foundations of masonry, 12 feet in depth. For greater strength, extra cement was added to the mortar binding the bricks. In order to provide still greater stability in case of an earthquake, the walls were reinforced every 4 feet with strips of iron, hammered out of 3,000 tons of scrap iron. (SFPL.)

At 5:12 a.m. on April 18, 1906, the San Andreas Fault slipped from Fort Bragg in Northern California to San Juan Batista in the south—a length of about 210 miles. The size of the quake was an estimated 8.3 on the Richter scale. (The Richter scale measures earthquakes on a scale of 10, with 10 being the most severe.) The epicenter of the earthquake was a few miles west of San Francisco, which kept the damage to the city from being even greater. Many locations to the north were damaged more severely than San Francisco. Nevertheless, San Francisco's streets buckled, cable car tracks were bent, chimneys and exterior walls fell, and many windows in the city were shattered. Gas pipelines and water mains were also broken. The greatest damage occurred in North Beach and the financial district, where swampy marshes and Yerba Buena Cove had been filled in during the Gold Rush. Another hard hit area was the civic center area, where the newly completed city hall, pictured here, collapsed. (SFPL.)

Because of its sturdy construction, the damage to the Palace Hotel was mostly cosmetic. There were cracks in the interior walls, falling plaster, and lots of broken glass, but no major structural damage. However, the nerves of the hotel guests were severely tested, and none more than those of famed tenor Enrico Caruso. Caruso had performed the role of Don Jose in the opera *Carmen* (right) and was a guest at the Palace Hotel. Tradition has it that he ran from the hotel in his nightshirt and a towel around his neck with an autographed portrait of Theodore Roosevelt under one arm. (The photograph below is from a reenactment at the anniversary of the earthquake.) He was heard to say, "Give me Vesuvius; San Francisco is an 'ell of a place." He vowed never to return to San Francisco, and he never did.

Despite the severity of the earthquake, it would prove to account for only about 20 percent of the damage to be inflicted on San Francisco during the next three days. When the earthquake struck, many of the city's residents were in the process of cooking breakfast with their wood-burning stoves. Many of the stoves were overturned by the earthquake, and hundreds of gas lanterns and candles fell to the floor. Many of the residents had fled from their homes when the earthquake began and were not inside to extinguish the fires in their infancy. Because the earthquake had ruptured many of the city's gas lines, this fuel was soon added to the fires already ignited. In the first half hour following the earthquake, over 50 fires were reported, many of them in the area south of Market Street, where most residences were made of wood. The first fires soon merged into one gigantic blaze south of Market where the Palace Hotel stood. The above photograph shows the fire consuming the Call Building, with the Palace on the extreme left.

Because of the history of fires in early San Francisco, the designers of the Palace Hotel demonstrated great foresight in the construction of firefighting systems in the hotel. The hotel had its own water supply with four artesian wells in the basement, with a capacity of providing 28,000 gallons per hour. The wells fed a reservoir in the basement, which held 675,000 gallons of water. There were also seven water tanks on the roof that could distribute 130,000 gallons of water under pressure provided by the hotel's own pumps. The emergency water supply was controlled by a separate distribution system, with 350 outlets and 20,000 feet of fire hose. Each room in the hotel was equipped with a fire detector, and watchmen patrolled the hallways every 30 minutes, day and night. Overall, the building was believed to be safe from a major fire.

The earthquake had also ruptured most of the city's water mains, so the firemen soon discovered they had no water with which to fight the fires. To make matters even worse, the San Francisco fire chief, Dennis Sullivan, was mortally wounded during the earthquake, so the job of fighting the fires and maintaining order in the city was assumed by the acting commander of the U.S. Army's Presidio of San Francisco, Gen. Frederick Funston. As the fire spread, the army decided to dynamite structures in the path of the flames in order to remove them as sources of firewood. Many believe this actually helped to spread the fire. However, by dynamiting scores of stately mansions along Van Ness Avenue, they were able to establish a firebreak along that broad avenue. Unfortunately, by this time, the bulk of downtown San Francisco had already been destroyed.

With their fire system undamaged by the earthquake, the hotel employees felt they could deal with the fire. The roof of the hotel was kept wet to prevent it from catching fire from burning embers raining down on it, and jets of water were sprayed on surrounding buildings. Onlookers on Nob Hill could see the flag on top of the hotel, and they began cheering each time it appeared through the smoke. However, by noon, the smaller fires south of Market Street had merged into one gigantic blaze, and by early afternoon, the hotel's reservoir had been pumped dry. At half past two, the Grand Hotel across the street had started to burn, and the last of the employees of the Palace Hotel were safely evacuated. The empty hotel was then destroyed, floor by floor, and finally, at 3:30 p.m., the flag vanished and the onlookers saw only a blackened pole.

After the three-day fire was finally extinguished, only the burned-out shell of the hotel remained, as shown in the photograph to the left. The photograph below shows the remains of the Palace and Grand Hotels in the foreground, with the shell of the Call Building reflected in the background.

After the fire, Lotta's Fountain became a rallying point for the people of San Francisco. (To the right is the fountain, along with the gutted remains of the Palace Hotel.) Family members would use the fountain as a meeting place or leave notes there to inform each other of where they were located. Each year since 1906, the survivors of the earthquake and fire gather at the fountain on April 18 at 5:12 a.m. to hold their annual commemoration. They are usually accompanied by scores of other observers, many dressed in Victorian costume. A total of 10 survivors participated in the centennial observance held on April 18, 2006.

In l a ct of the OIA Palace Hotel - the Market St. Portal.

Although the fire had completely gutted the first Palace Hotel, the superstructure remained virtually intact. Decisions had to be made as to whether a second hotel should be constructed and, if so, whether to tear down the remains of the first hotel or rebuild within the gutted superstructure. By this time, Bill Sharon had died, and ownership of the hotel had passed to his son, Fred. Fred Sharon opted to tear down the remains of the first Palace Hotel before constructing the successor hotel in the same location. Over 300 men worked day and night to accomplish the job, at a cost of $100,000. The demolition was even the subject of the postcard above. In the photograph on the right can be seen the last remaining portal of the first Palace Hotel. (Left, SFPL.)

Four

THE SECOND PALACE HOTEL

While the second Palace Hotel was being built, the Sharon family continued the hotel's tradition on a much smaller scale. On November 17, 1906, the Little Palace Hotel opened on the corner of Leavenworth and Post Streets, in downtown San Francisco (above). The hotel had 23 guest rooms, and its annex across the street contained another 23 rooms. The hotel existed for 251 days and had a total of 2,927 guests. (SFPL.)

Shown in the picture above, the large building on the left is the second Palace Hotel, being constructed in the midst of part of the rubble left from the 1906 earthquake and fire.

The second Palace Hotel, completed in 1909, is nine stories high and contains 550 rooms. By comparison, the original hotel was seven stories high with 880 rooms. The construction cost of the second hotel was $10 million, compared to $5 million for the first hotel in 1875. When the second hotel opened, its room rates were listed at $2 per night, compared to $1 for a room in the original hotel. The second hotel was designed by the New York firm of Trowbridge and Livingston, with George Kelham as the lead architect. Kelham remained in San Francisco after the completion of this project and went on to design numerous other classic San Francisco structures, including the Sharon Building, the Russ Building, the Security Pacific Bank, the Federal Reserve Bank, the J. Harold Dollar Building, the Standard Oil Building, the Shell Building, and the San Francisco Public Library.

2075 — PALACE HOTEL, SAN FRANCISCO, CALIFORNIA.

Although smaller than its predecessor, the second Palace Hotel shared the same footprint, which covers practically 2 acres in the heart of the city. The photograph above shows the second Palace Hotel. Pictured to the right is a view of the hotel at the center of the photograph, among other new buildings at the corner of Market, Post, and Montgomery Streets.

BANKING CENTER—MARKET, POST AND MONTGOMERY STREETS

The main entrance to the second Palace Hotel was located once again on New Montgomery Street. In place of the grand carriage entrance of the original Palace Hotel, guests were ushered through a revolving door into the lobby area, where they were greeted at the front desk. The above photograph shows the layout of the lobby in 1928. The photograph on the left, taken in 1930, shows the front desk and the hotel entrance as seen from the promenade.

The promenade of the second hotel runs the length of the building, from Market Street to Jessie Street. From the promenade, hotel guests have access to the lobby, the elevators, the Pied Piper Bar, the Ralston Room, and the Garden Court. The promenade has also gone through a series of changes over the years. Pictured in the above photograph is the flower stand, which used to fill the promenade with the aroma of fresh flowers. In the photograph below, virtually every inch of available space has been put to use.

On the evening of December 15, 1909, the second Palace Hotel opened with an all-male banquet. On the following day, the hotel was opened to the world by William Ralston's son, with a golden key. The key was taken to the roof, attached to five balloons, and when last seen was heading out through the Golden Gate. Ralston's was the first name on the hotel's register. That night, 1,500 members of San Francisco society turned out for the formal opening. The *San Francisco Chronicle* declared it to be "the world's record in number for service at small tables."

The most architecturally significant room in the second Palace Hotel is the world-famous Garden Court, which captures the splendor and tradition of the original hotel. The room occupies more than 8,000 square feet, making it one of the largest public rooms in the world. The domed ceiling, containing more than 70,000 pieces of colored glass, covers an area of 12,000 square feet, making it one of the largest expanses of colored glass in the world. The 20 chandeliers are made of Austrian crystal, and the 10 larger ones are approximately 6 feet tall, weigh about 750 pounds, and are valued at $50,000 each. The marble for the 16 Ionic columns came from Italy, as did the marble for the floor. Situated above the entrance to the room are the arched windows of the French Parlor.

The beauty of the Garden Court has also been the subject of numerous postcards, from the small table settings on the left to a massive banquet facility below.

The Palace Palm Court — The Most Beautiful Dining Room in America

Honoring President Wilson-1919

The Garden Court has been the site of countless grand occasions, none perhaps grander than the dinner hosted by Pres. Woodrow Wilson following World War I. The president was trying to persuade the country to join the League of Nations and closed his after-dinner speech by saying, "The League Of Nations is the world's greatest hope for peace." As he uttered the word "peace," a flock of doves were released from their cages in the French Parlor and flew into the Garden Court. Most circled the room and promptly returned to their cages in the French Parlor. A few, however, decided to remain in the Garden Court. After trying everything they could think of to coax the birds from the Garden Court, the hotel management finally hired hunters, with shotguns, and the "doves of peace" were removed. During the restoration, portions of the glass ceiling containing buckshot had to be replaced.

Although President Wilson was unable to get the United States into the League of Nations, the city of San Francisco played a major role in the creation of the United Nations following World War II. The United Nations Conference on International Organization was held in San Francisco from April 25, 1945, through June 26, 1945. The charter for the United Nations was completed in San Francisco, and the delegates to the U.N. Conference voted their approval of the charter in San Francisco's War Memorial Opera House. The official signing of the charter took place in the Herbst Theater of the War Memorial Veterans' Building on June 26. The above photograph depicts the dinner held in the Garden Court to celebrate the birth of the United Nations, with the delegates surrounded by the flags of the 50 nations that were charter members of the United Nations.

The hotel has also hosted numerous banquets to honor visiting dignitaries from other parts of the world. The photograph above shows another banquet in the Garden Court to celebrate the signing of the United Nations charter. In the photograph below are the state flags of Texas and California, which were both republics before being admitted to the union.

The Pied Piper Bar is named for the painting by Maxfield Parrish, considered the greatest commercial artist of his time. The Pied Piper painting was commissioned for the new hotel by Bill Sharon's son, Fred, after seeing a similar work by Parrish, the Old King Cole mural, in the Knickerbocker Hotel in New York City (above). Parrish was the highest paid commercial illustrator in the 1920s, using classical fine art themes in a commercial setting. Parrish was known as "the common man's Rembrandt" because so many people in America "owned" a work by Parrish, either on a calendar or an illustration in a children's book. Parrish's art featured dazzlingly luminous colors, including "Parrish blue," which was a unique blue coloring used in many of his skies.

The Piper painting is based on the children's fairy tale "The Pied Piper of Hamelin," where the Piper is leading a band of children away from their homes forever. Parrish did not like to use professional models as his subjects; he preferred to use "real people" instead. He used himself as the model for the Piper, and the children were some of those in his neighborhood. Two children (the one to the left of the piper and the one behind the rock) were his own. One of the women in the painting was his wife; another was his mistress. The painting was originally installed in the Palace Bar and then moved to the Rose Room during Prohibition. It was later moved to the Happy Valley Bar, now called the Pied Piper Bar.

Maxfield's is one of the three restaurants in the hotel today. It was originally a men's dining room; women were not allowed until the 1920s, after they received the right to vote. The floor of the restaurant is the original, made from marble mosaic tiles. The tiled floor was later covered by carpeting, which was affixed with glue. During the restoration of the hotel, the floor was uncovered and reconstructed, tile by tile. The ceiling of the restaurant was also reconstructed, after the original had been damaged by electrical, ventilation, and sprinkler construction and ultimately covered altogether with acoustic tiles. Because of breakage during the many renovations, only about 40 percent of the ceiling is the original glass; the rest was custom made during the restoration.

Featured within Maxfield's are two panels by Antonio Sotomayer portraying famous people from early San Francisco. Antonio Sotomayer immigrated to San Francisco from Bolivia and worked as a dishwasher in the hotel during the 1920s. He was fond of entertaining his coworkers with his doodles and caricatures, and they brought his talent to the attention of the hotel's owner, Janet Johnston, the granddaughter of Bill Sharon. Johnston commissioned Sotomayer to create the two panels. Sotomayer later attended art school and then taught art. Before his death, he was a member of the San Francisco Arts Commission. (SFPL.)

Among those featured in this panel is Mark Twain. Mark Twain moved to San Francisco from Virginia City in 1864 and supposedly said that "the coldest winter he ever spent was a summer in San Francisco." Beneath Twain's chair is the "celebrated jumping frog of Calaveras County," from one of his gold-country tales. The gentleman in the top hat is author Bret Harte, who also lived in San Francisco and worked with Mark Twain at the *Golden Era*, an early San Francisco newspaper. The gentleman with the cigar is Bill Sharon. Behind his head is a mask, which represents Sharon's poker face. Bill Sharon was reputed to be the best poker player on the West Coast. The "poker face" is holding a five-card poker hand, and all five cards are aces, which might reflect Sotomayer's opinion of Sharon's scruples. The gentleman in the uniform is Emperor Norton.

Joshua Norton came to San Francisco in 1849 and became a very successful businessman before he tried to corner the market on rice. When that failed, he lost everything, including perhaps his mind. When he was next seen in San Francisco, he was wearing a uniform and carrying a proclamation in his hand. Marching into the office of the editor of the *San Francisco Bulletin*, he threw the proclamation on the editor's desk and demanded he print it in his newspaper. The editor not only printed it; he put it on the front page, and Joshua Norton became a celebrity overnight. The proclamation declared him to be "Norton I: Emperor of the United States and Protector of Mexico." As the head of a sovereign nation, he was entitled to print his own money, which was accepted by the local merchants. (SPFL.)

Emperor Norton's job, as he saw it, was to make daily inspections of his realm and post public proclamations regarding improvements needed. Some of his proclamations actually made sense. He proclaimed that there should be a decorated Christmas tree in Union Square every December, and there has been one ever since. In 1869, he proposed, in the *Oakland Daily News*, the construction of a bridge between San Francisco and Oakland through Yerba Buena Island. Norton even wrote a check for the sum of $3 million to build the bridge, which was accomplished in 1936. He also wrote to President Lincoln to suggest that he divorce his wife and marry Queen Victoria. The president's personal secretary replied to the emperor that the president would give it every consideration. The emperor demanded, and was granted, a reserved seat in the visitor's gallery of the state senate and was greeted at every opening session as an honored guest. (SFPL.)

EMPEROR NORTON
— LUNCHING —
BUMMER & LAZARUS

The two dogs in the panel were named Bummer and Lazarus, and they followed Norton wherever he went. Whenever the San Francisco Opera opened its season, three tickets in the front-row balcony were always set aside for Norton, Bummer, and Lazarus. When a city ordinance was passed requiring dogs to be licensed and leashed, Bummer and Lazarus were specifically exempted by name. When Lazarus died, his body was stuffed and put on public display. The death of Bummer was the occasion for a eulogy by Mark Twain. There is still some question about whether the two dogs actually belonged to Emperor Norton. According to legend, the emperor once said that they were not his dogs, but they always accompanied him because they knew they would get a free handout. There were those who also accused Norton of the same strategy. However, when he died in 1890, the flag at city hall was lowered to half-staff, and his funeral cortege contained an estimated 30,000 people, the second largest funeral in San Francisco history. (SFPL.)

The man wearing the Colonial garb in this panel is "Uncle Freddy" Coombs. Coombs was a contemporary and obvious copycat of Emperor Norton and claimed to be the reincarnation of George Washington. Coombs would also post his own proclamations around town and eventually got into a proclamation war with Norton. They would tear down each other's proclamations and replace them with their own. Finally, Emperor Norton proclaimed that Coombs be placed in the state mental hospital. Coombs may have believed Norton had that kind of power, because he returned to New York shortly thereafter and was never seen again in San Francisco. The woman in the carriage is Lotta Crabtree.

Lotta Crabtree was raised in Grass Valley, California, and became the Shirley Temple of her day. Under the tutelage of an entertainer named Lola Montez, Lotta learned to sing and dance and became the darling of the gold miners. From there, she came to San Francisco to perform before sold-out crowds and then went on to great success in New York and Europe. At one time, she was the highest paid female entertainer in the world. However, she never forgot her roots in San Francisco and presented the city with a fountain on Market Street that still exists today. The dedication on the fountain reads, "Presented to the Citizens of San Francisco by Lotta—1875." Before there were Cher and Madonna, there was Lotta. (Both, SFPL.)

The Pied Piper painting (above) and the Sotomayer panels (below) were all displayed in the Happy Valley Bar at one time during the existence of the second hotel. (Both, SFPL.)

The talents of Antonio Sotomayer were also used by the hotel in other illustrations, such as the painting exhibited below. At the bottom of the floral arrangement on the poster to the right is the Sotomayer signature, to the left of the words "Sheraton Palace."

The French Parlor is located on the mezzanine level of the hotel, with windows overlooking the Garden Court. The room was originally used as a ladies' lounge and used to be known informally as the "fainting room." After couples had finished their dinner in the Garden Court, the gentlemen would remain behind to drink brandy, smoke cigars, and talk business. The ladies would be excused to go to the French Parlor to unwind. In those days, part of the unwinding process was loosening the ties on their corsets, which often caused a sudden rush of air that made them feel faint. Originally, the arches overlooking the Garden Court were open and later filled with wood panels painted on the outside to resemble the colored glass. During the restoration, the wooden panels were replaced with windows that can be open or closed, custom made to match the colored-glass canopy of the Garden Court. Today the French Parlor is used as a room for smaller meetings or luncheons.

It is believed by members of the hotel staff that the French Parlor might be inhabited by a ghost, who seems to like the isolation of that part of the hotel. While the rest of the hotel, including the French Parlor, was greatly disturbed during the restoration, the pantry adjacent to the French Parlor has been largely untouched since the hotel was built in 1909. It is there that a "feeling" has been reported, a feeling of being watched. People tell the story of the office manager who went alone to the French Parlor one night to look for a lost item. When finished with her task, she tried to leave through one of the doors, but it wouldn't budge. She then tried the other two exits, with the same result. Finally, pushing on one of the doors with all her might, it burst open, and she was pushed into the hallway by someone or something. She hurried back to her office, not daring to look back to see what might be there.

A total of 13 U.S. presidents have stayed in the hotel's Presidential Suite. They were George H. W. Bush, Grover Cleveland, Ulysses S. Grant, Warren G. Harding, Benjamin Harrison, Rutherford B. Hayes, William McKinley, Franklin D. Roosevelt, Theodore Roosevelt, William Howard Taft, and Woodrow Wilson. Pictured above is Pres. Gerald Ford in the 1970s.

Another big-name president to grace the hotel is the late John F. Kennedy, shown here at an unidentified function in the early 1960s.

In January 1891, King David Kalakaua of Hawaii stopped at the hotel. Although he was quite ill at the time of his arrival, he attended a number of social engagements in San Francisco, including dinner at the Bohemian Club and lunch with John D. Spreckels, who was interested in growing sugar cane in Hawaii. After leaving San Francisco, his health grew worse, and he returned to San Francisco. Against the advice of his doctors, he insisted on attending two additional social functions. These were his last public appearances. On January 20, 1891, the last king of Hawaii passed away, and the Hawaiian flag above the Palace Hotel was lowered to half-mast.

Among the celebrities who have graced the Palace Hotel are crooner Bing Crosby (second from right) and comedian Phil Harris (right) in the photograph above, and the very dapper Lucius Beebe, standing beside a golden ice bucket in the Garden Court to the right. (Right, SFPL.)

World-famous sports legends have also been seen within the hotel. In the photograph on the left, former St. Louis Cardinal and Hall of Famer Stan "The Man" Musial is seen enjoying a cup of coffee in one of the hotel's dining rooms. In the photograph below, another Hall of Famer, Ted Williams (closest to the camera at left) of the Boston Red Sox, is partaking of a Sunday brunch in the Garden Court.

Among the famous banquets held in the hotel was the Friends of the Comstock Lode dinner in 1876, where the menu for the 11-course banquet was engraved on solid silver. In 1915, the menu for a dinner honoring Thomas Edison was written in Morse code. In 1927, Charles Lindbergh was honored at a dinner to celebrate his crossing of the Atlantic. In 1959, USSR premier Nikita Krushchev addressed the World Affairs Council and the Commonwealth Club at a dinner in the Garden Court. Finally, in 1960, President Eisenhower was honored in the Garden Court, as shown in the photograph below. Above, Ike is shown entering the Garden Court.

Honoring President Eisenhower - 1960

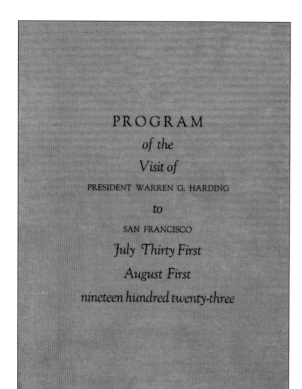

PROGRAM

of the

Visit of

PRESIDENT WARREN G. HARDING

to

SAN FRANCISCO

July Thirty First

August First

nineteen hundred twenty-three

In July 1923, the 29th president of the United States, Warren G. Harding, arrived at the hotel at the conclusion of an Alaskan cruise. The president was sick upon his arrival in San Francisco. His two White House doctors diagnosed him with ptomaine poisoning from bad clams on the Alaska cruise and advised rest until he was well enough to return to Washington. Harding was in bed by 7:00 p.m. on August 2, and his wife, Florence, was reading to him. At 7:35 p.m., when one of the White House doctors arrived, Harding's dead body was lying on top of the bed. After Florence Harding refused to allow an autopsy, the doctors announced that the president had died from a stroke. The program heralding Harding's visit is displayed above, while the photograph below shows the menu and other memorabilia prepared for his state dinner.

The photograph above, taken before the day of the cell phone, shows the hotel's early communications center. Located adjacent to the lobby, the room contained two banks of private phone booths, and calls were directed by a staff of three telephone operators. As shown below, the hotel also contained a barbershop at one time. Keeping in the grandiose tradition of the hotel, the barbershop contained 17 chairs, with 20 barbers and manicurists to meet the needs of the guests and other clientele. (Below, SFPL.)

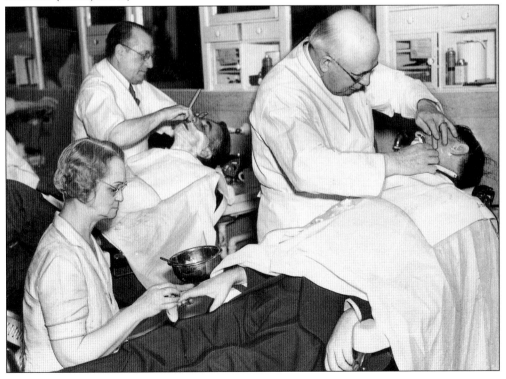

Lotta's Fountain, Palace Hotel, San Francisco

Throughout its history, fine food has been a hallmark of the hotel. While the quality of the cuisine has remained at the same high level, the names and locations of the cafés and dining rooms have changed over the years. Gone are the Tudor Room, the Minute Chef, the Happy Valley Bar, and Lotta's Fountain, with the latter's name being a whimsical takeoff on the original Lotta's Fountain located on Market Street, just outside the door of the café. Pictured above is a photograph of Lotta's Fountain, which also featured murals painted by Antonio Sotomayer. Shown below is a composite image of current and past hotel dining areas.

82

Cocktails

Avocado, Grapefruit 90	Olympia Oysters 1.85	Crab 1.40
Shrimp 1.35	Fresh Fruit Cup 95	Prawns 1.70
Crab Legs 1.85		Lobster 2.25

Oysters

Blue Points on Half Shell 2.25   Baked Kirkpatrick 2.60   Blue Points, Fried 2.50
Milk Stew—Eastern Oysters 2.00; Olympia Oysters 2.75

Hors D'Oeuvre

Assorted Hors d'Oeuvre Palace 2.25	Avocado Gourmet 2.60
Smoked Salmon 1.85	Grapefruit Alice 75	Caviar on Ice 4.60
Green & Ripe Olives 65	Stuffed Celery Roquefort 1.10	Celery & Olives 90
Pate Maison 1.40	Escargots Burguignonne 2.60

Prosciutto Ham with Melon or Papaya 2.20

Soups

CREAM OF CELERY BALSAC 45	CONSOMME CARMEN 45
Chicken Broth 60	Beef Consomme 60	Cream Tomato 75

Cold: Jellied Chicken Broth or Madrilene 70
Cream Vichyssoise or Senegalaise 70

Fish and Seafood

BROOK TROUT SAUTE CAPRICE 3.25
FILETS OF REX SOLE AMANDINE, POTATO WINDSOR 2.40
BAKED STUFFED LOBSTER THERMIDOR 3.25
COQUILLE OF CRAB LEGS DEWEY 2.75
FILETS OF ENGLISH SOLE, NORMANDE 2.75
PANFRIED ABALONE, BELLE MEUNIERE 2.75

From the Charcoal Broiler

FILET MIGNON 5.00	NEW YORK SIRLOIN STEAK 5.00
TOP SIRLOIN STEAK 3.50	FRENCH LAMB CHOP (2) 3.50
ENGLISH LAMB CHOPS MIXED GRILL 4.00	
CHATEAU BRIAND (for 2) 10.00	MINUTE SIRLOIN STEAK 4.25
DOUBLE NEW YORK STEAK, BEARNAISE SAUCE 12.00	
HALF SPRING CHICKEN AND BACON, MAITRE 'D 2.35	
GENUINE SQUAB A LA CRAPAUDINE 4.00	
CHOPPED TENDERLOIN STEAK, FRIED ONIONS 2.50	
HAM STEAK 2.95	

Grilled Tomato, Mushroom Head and Julienne Potato served with all Steaks and Chops

Cold Buffet

Steak Tartare 3.00	Roast California Turkey 2.50
Baked Sugar Cured Ham 2.50	Smoked Ox Tongue 1.95
Roast Prime Ribs of Beef 3.95	Assorted Cold Cuts 2.75
Avocado with Chicken Salad 2.35	Brisket of Corned Beef 2.35

Garden Court Dinner

MONDAY, JUNE 22, 1959

Cocktails

Manhattan 75	Old Fashioned 75
Martini 75	Daiquiri 80

Today's Sheraton Chef's Special
3.00
BEEF TENDERLOIN EN BROCHETTE
(Tender beef cubes and bacon squares with mushroom caps broiled to your liking. Served on toast, accompanied by Delmonico potatoes and new peas.)

Entrees

INCLUDES CRISP GREEN SALAD WITH FRENCH DRESSING OR SOUP DU JOUR

SUPREME OF HALIBUT IN BORDURE NORMANDE 2.50

VEAL CUTLET "CORDON BLEU" STUFFED WITH HAM AND SWISS CHEESE, FRESH ASPARAGUS 3.25

SPRING LAMB CHOPS SOUBISE, BROCCOLI AU GRATIN 2.75

BONED SQUAB CHICKEN IN CASSEROLE FORRESTIERE 3.25

ROAST PRIME RIBS OF BEEF, BAKED IDAHO POTATO 4.20

ROAST CALIFORNIA TURKEY, ENGLISH DRESSING, SWEET POTATO, CRANBERRY SAUCE 2.75

BREAD AND BUTTER 20

THE FLAMING SPECIALTY
3.70
LOBSTER A LA BEEBE
FLAMBE WITH WHISKEY AT YOUR TABLE

Substitutions Subject to Additional Charge

In addition to the prices quoted above, there are state and city taxes aggregating 4%

Salads

Original Palace Court with: Crab 2.70	Chicken 2.70	Bay Shrimp 2.50
Green Goddess 90	with: Crab 2.80	Chicken 2.80	Bay Shrimp 2.40

Chef's Salad: Crisp Mixed Greens with Julienne Chicken, Turkey, Tongue, Cheese 2.10

Hearts of Lettuce 60	Heart of Romaine 70	Fresh Fruit 1.60
Mixed Green 70	Sliced Tomato 75	Fresh Vegetables 95

(The above are served with Cal. French or Thousand Island Dressing)

Vegetables - Potatoes

Cauliflower 65; with Hollandaise 95		New Lima Beans 55
String Beans 60	Assorted Vegetable Plate 1.95	Garden Peas 50
Heart of Artichoke Saute 95		English Spinach 45
Baked 50	French Fried 45 Mashed 45	Hashed Brown 50
Au Gratin 60	Lyonnaise 50	Long Branch 50

Palace Pastries and Desserts

PIES: Honey Apple, Peach, Palace Strawberry 50

Gateau Nicoise 60	Mocha Layer Cake 50
Hawaiian Shortcake 55	Apricot Rice Pudding 50
Fresh Fruit Macerated in White Wine 75	Palace Nut Cake 75
Baba au Rhum 1.00	Peach Flambé au Grand Marnier 1.75

Ice Cream

Coupe Rose Marie 60	Chocolate Parfait 65	Strawberry Sundae 75
Pear Cardinal 90		Marshmallow Sundae 60

Palace Black Walnut Ice Cream 65

Praline Ice Cream 65	Palace Strawberry Sherbet 70

Pistachio, Strawberry, Chocolate, Mocha or Vanilla 50

Chocolate Roll Glace 90	Raspberry Water Ice 45 Frozen Eggnog 80

Fruits in Season

Banana with Cream 80	Papaya 80	Half Grapefruit 50
Cantaloupe 55	Crenshaw 65	Fresh Strawberries 85

Cheese

American 45	Imported Swiss 60	Monterey Cream 60	Bleu 55 Cottage 45
Philadelphia Cream 60	Brie 70	Liederkranz 65	Camembert 65

Coffee, Tea, Etc.

Coffee, Pot 50	Demi Tasse 35	French Special 55
Cafe Expresso 65	Iced Tea or Iced Coffee 50	Buttermilk 55
Milk 30		English, Ceylon or Orange Pekoe Tea 40

We Suggest...

Palace Hotel Claret or Sauterne
1/2 Bottle 1.25   Bottle 2.00

The Garden Court menu above reflects prices in 1959, not those of today.

Famous Palace Hotel Recipes

Famous Recipes: **Green Goddess Dressing - A Palace Original**

Created between 1915 and 1920 by Palace Chef Philip Roemer in honor of actor George Arliss, who was staying at the Palace while starring in William Archer's play titled "The Green Goddess"

8 to 10 fillets of anchovies

1 green onion

½ cup fine cut chives

2 tablespoons minced tarragon

1/4 cup minced parsley

½ cup tarragon vinegar

3 cups mayonnaise

lettuce: romaine, escarole & chicory

Mince anchovies with green onion. Add minced parsley and minced tarragon, mayonnaise, tar-
and tarragon vinegar and finely cut chives.

Cut romaine, escarole and chicory. Mix dressing and greens together in a bowl that has
been rubbed with garlic.

(The salad may be topped with chicken, crab or shrimp).

AN ITT SHERATON LUXURY HOTEL.

2 New Montgomery Street • San Francisco, CA 94105-3402 • (415) 392-8600 • Fax (415) 243-8062

One of the culinary delights created at the hotel is the Green Goddess dressing. Actor George
Arliss was staying at the hotel while starring in the play entitled *The Green Goddess.* Evidently
he did not care for any of the salad dressings available at the hotel and challenged the chef,
Philip Roemer, to come up with something better. The recipe for Green Goddess dressing is
shown above.

The Palace Hotel is also famous for its legendary buffets. The photograph above shows the final touches being made for a buffet in the hotel ballroom. Today the famed Garden Court brunch is featured on Sundays, as depicted in the photograph below.

ANSON WEEKS AND HIS ORCHESTRA

THE SHERATON-PALACE HONORS ANSON WEEKS

ON THE

FIFTIETH YEAR OF "DANCIN' WITH ANSON"

MENU

LA CHIFFONNADE DE LAITUES A LA NORMANDE

•

LE COEUR DE CELERIS EN BRANCHE
LES OLIVES VERTES ET NOIRES

LA COTE DE BOEUF ROTI SAUCE RAIFORT
LES HARICOTS VERTS AUX CHAMPIGNONS
LES POMMES AU FOUR A L'ANGLAISE

•

LES PETITS PAINS OPERA
LE BEURRE DE FERME

•

LE PARGAIT AU MOKA
LES PETITS FOURS ET LES CAROLINES

•

LE CAFE OU LE THE DU PALACE

GARDEN COURT, TUESDAY, MAY 23, 1967
MORGAN J. SMITH, General Manager

Dancing has been one of the proudest traditions of the Palace Hotel. Over the course of its history, dances have been held in virtually every ballroom in the hotel, including the Garden Court. The most enduring tradition was dancing to the music of big band leader Anson Weeks. "Dancin' with Anson" was a tradition that endured for more than 50 years. In the above photograph of Anson and his orchestra, notice the two microphones that broadcast the music live on radio station KFRC. The flyer on the left celebrated the golden anniversary of "Dancin' with Anson."

Other big bands also appeared in the ballrooms of the hotel. The flyer shown above promotes an event with Desi Arnaz and his orchestra in the Rose Room. Pictured below is a flyer advertising the appearance of the Norval Knight Orchestra in the Garden Court. Note that a charge of $1 was levied for dancing, except on Saturdays, when it escalated to $1.50.

The second editions of both the Palace Hotel and the Grand Hotel have been celebrated by postcards. The Grand Hotel is illustrated in the image above, and the second Palace Hotel is shown in its environs below.

While the guest rooms of the second hotel lacked the royal splendor of those in the original version, they nevertheless meet the standards expected of a luxury hotel, as revealed in the photographs from the 20th century above and the deluxe suite parlor of today.

Ownership of the second hotel remained with descendants of Bill Sharon until 1954, when the Sheraton Corporation acquired it from Mrs. William Johnston (Janet), Sen. William Sharon's granddaughter. The hotel was then known as the Sheraton-Palace until purchased by Hawaiian-based Kyo-Ya Hotels and Resorts. Today the hotel is managed by Starwood Hotels and Resorts, which manages luxury hotels around the world. At left, the Sheraton Palace sign sits on top of the hotel. Today it reads "The Palace." Because the hotel has been designated a San Francisco Historic Landmark, it had to make the word "the" from the letters of the former word "Sheraton." Below is the hotel's entrance as the Sheraton-Palace. (Left, SFPL.)

Throughout its history, the hotel has been a major site for meetings in San Francisco. Pictured above is a photograph from a 1949 Studebaker gathering, and below is a session promoting Hawaii.

Numerous other conferences have been held at the hotel, including a dinner to celebrate the 1915 World's Fair (above) and a convention of businessmen (below). (Both, SFPL.)

The hotel becomes even more beautiful and magical during the holidays. The photograph above shows the Garden Court enhanced by a gigantic Christmas tree, and the Grand Ballroom below has been transformed into a winter wonderland.

New Year's Eve has also been the occasion for revelry at the hotel, both on the dance floor above and at the dinner tables below. (Both, SFPL.)

The arrival of the spring season has also been the occasion for festivity. In the photograph above, a pair of Easter bunnies are gathering eggs, while the children on the right are about to be rewarded by a third member of the bunny corps.

Other seasonal events celebrated at the hotel have been the Mardi Gras shown above and the opening of the yacht season depicted below. According to newspaper accounts, the Mardi Gras Ball was sponsored by the San Francisco Spinsters, and the dancing began at 10:30 and continued until well after dawn.

Other cultural events that have been celebrated at the hotel have been the Finnish Ball above and a good old-fashioned barn dance (below).

Lotta's Fountain Palace Hotel San Francisco

The second Palace Hotel has been the subject of countless postcards sent from elated guests to their envious friends. Pictured above is a postcard of Lotta's Fountain. Shown below is a beautiful rendering of the appeal of the hotel, from the early pioneer days to the vision of the current hotel.

AT THE END OF THE TRAIL STANDS THE PALACE HOTEL — SAN FRANCISCO

The hotel has also been the scene for a number of movies made in San Francisco. In *Herbie Rides Again*, Herbie the Love Bug drives through the Garden Court. In *Jade* (1995), David Caruso is seen dancing at the Black and White Ball. Caruso rushes out of the ballroom to make a phone call, and viewers get a glance of the Pied Piper painting in the hotel's bar. In a scene from *The Game* (1997), Michael Douglas tries to kill himself by jumping off the roof of the hotel. He crashes through the glass ceiling of the Garden Court, and to his astonishment (and that of the audience), he lands on a pillow and finds himself at his own surprise birthday party.

As the main street of San Francisco, Market Street has been the primary parade route for the city. Since each of the two Palace Hotels had one side facing Market Street, the hotel's guests have had a prime vantage point for these events, both joyous and otherwise. In the photograph above is the first Palace Hotel during a parade held in 1904. Nineteen years later, on a more somber occasion, the funeral cortege of President Harding would follow the same route up Market Street to the train station, where his body was sent on to the nation's capitol. (SFPL.)

Some of the better suites in the second hotel are even more luxurious than their counterparts in the earlier version of the hotel. Pictured at right is the sitting room of the former Governor's Suite, contrasted with today's Ambassador Suite shown in the photograph below.

Originally, a few suites on the Market Street side of the hotel had small balconies, as shown in the photograph above. During the 1950s, the balconies were removed because of deterioration, as reflected in the photograph below.

Five

THE PALACE HOTEL RESTORED

To restore the second Palace Hotel to its 1909 splendor, the hotel was closed for renovation in January 1989. On October 17, 1989, the San Francisco Bay area was struck by another major earthquake, the Loma Prieta Earthquake. Unlike the first Palace Hotel, the second version suffered major structural damage. The damage was so severe that work on the restoration was halted, and a whole new repair and restoration contract was completed. As a result, the hotel did not reopen until April 1991, and the total cost for the restoration exceeded $150 million.

During the restoration of the hotel, the Garden Court was lovingly restored to its original grandeur, with special attention paid to the room's legendary $7-million stained-glass ceiling. Each and every one of the more than 70,000 pieces of glass was removed, cleaned, and reset with zinc, providing more stability than the original lead. Damaged pieces were either repaired or replaced with new ones, custom made to match the original design. The restoration of the ceiling took approximately one year to complete, at a cost in excess of $1 million. The photograph above shows the dome without its glass, while the workers at left appear to be dancing with joy as they install the panes of glass.

The Garden Court contains pairs of marble columns, as shown in both photographs. When first constructed, only one column of each pair was made of solid marble. Each mate was reinforced by a steel beam connected to a girder above. During the 1989 earthquake, the non-reinforced columns were damaged by the quake and were rebuilt with steel beams inserted into both columns. Portions of the marble floor of the Garden Court in the photograph to the right were also damaged by the quake, and replacement marble was shipped from the original quarry in Italy.

The Conference Center, located on the second floor, was added during the remodeling of the hotel in 1989. Previously, the space had been occupied by a local radio station. The central area is covered by a galleria ceiling, which allows sunlight to stream into the area. In order to keep the area from becoming a hot house, approximately half of the glass is covered by a ceramic material baked onto the glass itself. This material was first developed for the National Aeronautics and Space Administration in order to reduce the amount of heat on space shuttles as they reenter the earth's atmosphere. Approximately 50 percent of the glass is covered by the ceramic, thus reflecting 50 percent of the sun's rays. In the photograph below, workers are shown installing the windowpanes.

Before embarking on the restoration, the preservation architects spent two years researching the 1909 hotel. The photograph to the right shows the appearance of the promenade after the restoration. The walls of the promenade are plaster painted with a "shadow glaze" to make them look like stone. The throne chairs have been part of the hotel since about 1910. In the photograph below, workers are shown in the restoration process.

Following the restoration of the Garden Court, the hotel also reinstituted the tradition of the afternoon tea. Guests can choose from traditional and exotic blends of tea, accompanied by classic tea sandwiches, delicate pastries and scones, and fresh seasonal fruit. Guests can also enjoy breakfast, lunch, and dinner in the Garden Court today. Highlighting the menu are early San Francisco favorites developed by Palace chefs during the late 1800s and early 1900s.

Two of the most beautiful features of Maxfield's restaurant are the marble mosaic floor and the stained-glass ceiling. Sometime between 1909 and 1989, a carpet was glued to the floor, and an acoustical ceiling was installed over the original stained-glass panels in the ceiling. After the carpet was removed during the restoration, every one of the floor tiles had to be removed, cleaned, and reset. Because many of the stained-glass panels were damaged when the acoustical ceiling was installed, custom stained-glass panels were made to replace the originals.

A bouquet of fresh flowers greets the guests. It sits on a table of rosso levanto marble with a carved wood base and 22-carat accents. The center of the foyer has an eight-pointed marble star that was originally a pattern in the revolving entrance of 1910 and was rediscovered during the restoration. The custom-designed torchieres provide uplight and accent architectural elements at each entrance. They are constructed of bronze with carved alabaster bowls.

During the remodeling, an indoor swimming pool and a fitness center were added to the hotel. Notice the galleria ceiling over the pool, mimicking that of the Conference Center.

In the Promenade, the leaded-glass ceiling panels were restored and are illuminated by a computer-controlled system that can be set at a variety of modes to simulate different times of the day. The plaster walls are original but were extensively repaired. New marble floors were constructed throughout the hotel based on the original working drawings of 1910. The two massive oak throne chairs shown in the photograph above were present when the hotel opened in 1909. At 71 inches high, 32 inches wide, and 28 inches deep, the chairs offer a welcome resting place to hotel visitors.

The walls of the registration area are made of African and Honduran mahogany. The front desk is also mahogany, with a verde patricia marble counter. Note the galleria ceiling over the front desk, again mimicking the ceiling in the Conference Center and the Garden Court dome. The carpet was custom made and woven on Axminster looms in England. The carpet pattern was designed for the hotel using the original hotel logo embraced by the Sheraton wreath. The painting behind the clerk at the front desk features the original Palace Hotel in 1875.

The Grand Ballroom was originally the Ladies' Dining Room, as was the custom of the times. The Grand Ballroom is comprised of the Rose Room and Concert Room and features removable walls for smaller and larger group events. At its fullest, the room can accommodate 1,200 guests. The original room had glass skylights, which were removed with the addition of the Sunset Court and Conference Center in the floor above. In place of the skylights, a new ceiling was constructed, which contains 1,500 feet of classically detailed frieze work. The new ceiling took five months to create. The chandeliers are made of Austrian crystal. The photograph to the left shows the ballroom as it appeared in 1923, and below is the Grand Ballroom today.

The Gold Ballroom has also been restored to its original splendor. Throughout its history, this room has been the scene of banquets, dances, balls, and wedding receptions. During the restoration, the gold leaf and the musical motif were painstakingly brought back to life. As seen in the above photograph, the room even retains its original fireplace, although it is no longer used today. The photograph at right shows the beautifully restored musical motif.

The hotel's 550 guest rooms and suites have been completely renovated and elegantly refurbished, with all of the rooms retaining their high ceilings and general spaciousness. The photograph above shows one of the suites from earlier years, with a comparable room of today portrayed in the photograph below.

One of the hotel's logos shows the head of a lion at the top of a shield containing the letters PH intertwined with each other. The photograph above shows this image, which appears over the hotel's main entrance, after it was meticulously restored in 1989. To the right, the same lion's head appears on one of the lamps in the lobby.

PALACE HOTEL
San Francisco

The phoenix is utilized as another logo of the hotel. The phoenix is a mythical sacred firebird in ancient Phoenician mythology. It is said to have a 500-year life cycle, and near the end of that period, it ignites itself in its own nest and emerges from the ashes as a new, young phoenix. The bird is also said to regenerate when wounded by a foe, thus being almost immortal. The symbolism obviously fits the hotel, which was destroyed in the fire of 1906 only to be reborn in its second version. The second hotel was also wounded by the 1989 earthquake and again emerged in all of its original splendor after the restoration The logo appears frequently on hotel publications, as shown above, and also whimsically, as with the cake decoration below.

From the time the hotel opened in 1909, the Garden Court chandeliers had never been removed for cleaning prior to the restoration. In the photograph below, a hotel employee is shown on a ladder, cleaning each of the chandeliers by hand. Today the Garden Court is closed for one week annually while the chandeliers are sprayed and allowed to drip-dry.

As a result of the 1989 earthquake, additional seismic upgrading was performed during the restoration. Concrete shear walls were added to the back of the building to complement those that had been added previously. Resting on a 24-inch granite foundation, the building has a steel frame which can move and then return to its original configuration during an earthquake. The exterior walls of the hotel were also completely restored. As shown in the photograph above, the hotel's exterior is made of Utah limestone up to the second-floor window level and pressed brick from there on.

The Pied Piper Bar was also relocated during the restoration. The original Pied Piper Bar, in the above photograph, was located in the space where Maxfield's restaurant is today. The Pied Piper Bar today is located in the area formerly occupied by the Happy Valley Bar, pictured below.

The Pied Piper painting is once again the focal point of the bar that bears its name. During the restoration period, the painting was moved to the de Young Museum for display and safekeeping. When last appraised, the painting was valued at $2.5 million. The painting was originally commissioned for the sum of $20,000 in 1909.

The Conference Center contains a series of smaller meeting rooms that can be used in conjunction with or in lieu of the larger meeting rooms on the first floor. Shown in the above photograph is the Montgomery Room, and below is the Twin Peaks room. Each of the meeting rooms adjacent to the Sunset Court are named after neighborhoods in San Francisco.

Two former restaurants that used to exist within the hotel were the Minute Chef (above), which was open for breakfast and lunch, and the Tudor Room (at left), which catered to the dinner crowd. Both of these eateries shared the same kitchen, and both are now the sites of retail outlets.

APPENDIX
PALACE HOTEL
GUESTS THROUGH THE YEARS

Konrad Adenauer—chancellor of West Germany
Henry Ward Beecher—clergyman, editor, and abolitionist
King Albert and Queen Elizabeth of Belgium
Sarah Bernhardt—actress
Milton Berle—entertainer
Prince Napoleon Louis Joseph Jerome Bonaparte
Don Pedro II—Emperor of Brazil
Princess Louise, Duchess of Argyll—daughter of Queen Victoria
Former President and First Lady George H. W. and Barbara Bush
William Jennings Bryan—attorney and political leader
Adm. Richard Byrd—naval officer and polar explorer
Andrew Carnegie—industrialist and philanthropist
Enrico Caruso—Italian-born opera singer
Charlie (Sir Charles Spencer) Chaplin—actor, director, producer
Madame Chaing Kai-Shek of China
Lord and Lady Randolph Churchill of Great Britain
Winston Churchill—British prime minister
Pres. Grover Cleveland
First Lady Hillary Rodham Clinton
Bing Crosby—entertainer
Mario Cuomo—governor of New York
Amelia Earhardt—aviator
Sir Robert Anthony Eden—British prime minister
Thomas Edison—inventor
Harvey Firestone—industrialist
Marshal of France Ferdinand Foch
William H. Gates III, chief executive officer and chairman of Microsoft
Whoopi Goldberg—actress and comedian
Al and Tipper Gore—vice president and "second lady"
Pres. Ulysses S. Grant
Prince Phillip of Great Britain
Pres. Warren G. Harding (died here)

Pres. Benjamin Harrison
King David Kalakaua of Hawaii (died here)
Lady Drummond Hay (first woman to travel around the world by zeppelin)
Pres. Rutherford B. Hayes
Anna Held—French-born entertainer
Princess Juliana of Holland
Chief Justice Oliver Wendell Holmes Jr.
Marshal of France Joseph Jacques Joffre
Nikita Krushchev—Soviet premier
Fiorello H. La Guardia—mayor of New York
Sir Harry Lauder—Scottish singer and songwriter
D. H. Lawrence—English novelist
Ferdinand de Lessups—French diplomat
Count Giorgis Eurico Levi—world's premier fencing authority
Sir Thomas Lipton—Scottish-born businessman and philanthropist
Sophia Loren—Italian actress
Guglielmo Marconi—Italian inventor
Gen. George B. McClellan—Civil War general, politician
Col. John McCormick—newspaper publisher
Pres. William McKinley
Ed McMahon—entertainer
Joe Montana—football player
John Pierpont Morgan—industrialist
Lord and Lady Louis Mountbatten of Great Britain
Queen Juliana of the Netherlands
Prince Olav and Princess Martha of Norway
Ross Perot—investor, presidential candidate
George M. Pullman—industrialist, Pullman trains
Robert Reich—secretary of commerce (Clinton administration)
John David Rockefeller—industrialist
Ginger Rogers—entertainer
Will Rogers—author, actor
Pres. Franklin Delano Roosevelt
Pres. Theodore Roosevelt (during campaign)
Lillian Russell—entertainer
Grand Duchess Marie of Russia
Prince Louis of Savoy
Ridley Scott—film director
John Scully—former chairman, Apple Computer
Gen. William T. Sherman—Civil War general
George Schultz—secretary of state (Nixon administration)
C. Kingsford Smith—Australian aviator
Col. Charles Stanton (originated the saying "Lafayette, we are here.")
Clement Studebaker—industrialist
Pres. William Howard Taft
Mark Twain—author
Jimmy Walker—mayor of New York
Oscar Wilde—Irish poet, playwright
Wendell Willke—American politician
Pres. Woodrow Wilson
King Alexander of Yugoslavia

BIBLIOGRAPHY

Adams, Charles F. *The Magnificent Rogues of San Francisco*. Palo Alto, CA: Pacific Books, 1998.

Alexander, James Beach, and James Lee Heig. *San Francisco, Building the Dream City*. San Francisco: Scottwall Associates, 2002.

Brechin, Gray. *Imperial San Francisco*. Berkeley: University of California Press, 1999.

Bronson, William. *The Earth Shook, the Sky Burned*. San Francisco: Chronicle Books, 1997.

Cass, Maxine. *It Happened in San Francisco*. Guilford, CT: Morris Book Publishing, 2006.

Cole, Tom. *A Short History of San Francisco*. San Francisco: Don't Call It Frisco Press, 1988.

Dana, Julian. *The Man Who Built San Francisco*. New York: The Macmillan Company, 1937.

Hall, Carroll D., and Oscar Lewis. *Bonanza Inn*. New York: Alfred A. Knopf, 1939.

Lavender, David. *Nothing Seemed Impossible*. Palo Alto, CA: American West Publishing Company, 1975.

Lewis, Oscar. *Silver Kings*. New York: Alfred A. Knopf, 1964.

Richards, Rand. *Historic San Francisco*. San Francisco: Heritage House, 1991.

Shank, Will, and Jim Van Buskirk. *Celluloid San Francisco*. Chicago: Chicago Review Press, 2006.

Starr, Kevin. *California: A History*. New York: The Modern Library, 2005.

Discover Thousands of Local History Books Featuring Millions of Vintage Images

Arcadia Publishing, the leading local history publisher in the United States, is committed to making history accessible and meaningful through publishing books that celebrate and preserve the heritage of America's people and places.

Find more books like this at
www.arcadiapublishing.com

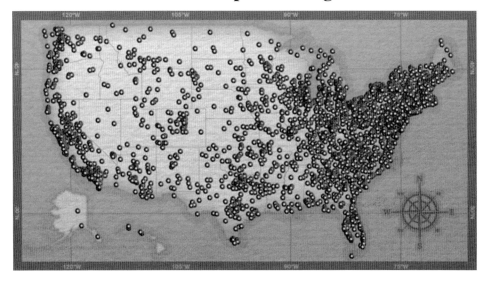

Search for your hometown history, your old stomping grounds, and even your favorite sports team.